The Jungle Group

Conversations you never hear

Prashant Padwal

BookLeaf Publishing

India | USA | UK

Made with ❤ on the BookLeaf Publishing Platform
www.bookleafpub.in
www.bookleafpub.com

Dedication

Dedicated to the incredible inhabitants of the jungle, whose lives and voices inspire these pages, and to the silent ones whose stories remain untold. This book is for the wild, the free, and the forgotten, and for all who strive to protect the world we share.

Also, dedicated to my father, who passed away last year. His love, wisdom, and memory continue to guide me every day.

Preface

"The Jungle Group : Conversations you never hear" is a collection of poems that invites you to eavesdrop on the conversations of the jungle's incredible inhabitants, each speaking in their own voice, yet united by one common theme: the changing world they call home.

The animals—so often viewed as silent witnesses to humanity's relentless progress—now speak out. In these verses, they share their stories of survival, loss, adaptation, and, most poignantly, the impact of human presence that has reshaped their existence. Through these conversations, you will encounter a new perspective on the jungle—a place not just of beauty, but of profound fragility.

As you journey through the pages of this book, listen closely to the voices of the jungle. These conversations are more than stories; they are urgent calls for awareness, for compassion, for understanding.

May these poems open your eyes and hearts to the voices of the voiceless, and inspire you to walk more gently on this Earth, as we are all, in the end, inhabitants of the same world.

Acknowledgements

I am deeply grateful to all the voices of the incredible inhabitants of the jungle whose lives and struggles I've tried to capture in these pages. Though they may not speak as humans do, their stories are no less important, and I hope I've done justice to their wisdom.

I owe a special thanks to the conservationists, wildlife researchers, and environmental advocates whose tireless efforts to protect our planet have inspired me so much. Their work reminds me that the jungle is not just a place of beauty, but a fragile ecosystem in need of our care. This book stands as a small tribute to their dedication.

I also wish to thank my family and friends, for their unwavering support and also thanks to the publishers for bringing this book from idea to reality.

Finally, **"A Big Thank You"** to all my readers. I am deeply grateful to each of you who takes the time to listen, to reflect, and to engage with the spirit of the jungle in this collection.

1. Trees :

On this place, for decades we stand,
Me and my friends, from sacred land.
Old and wise, we stand tall and free,
Scrawny calls this place a Jungle,
And then we are called its Trees.

Our branches stretch, to touch the sky.
Our roots run deep, where secrets lie.
Treasure troves or bodies buried,
Fruits of their fate or work of their greed.

We've witnessed all stories,
Yet never intervened.
But times are now changed,
So let our discussions begin.

We welcome you all, as today's host,
Feel free to express and put all your quotes.
Lets hear from you all, may take some notes,
And finish our meet, before Scrawny turns us to boats!

2. Mammoth :

Here I am, the oldest,
Yearning to say out first.
As I had lost my body,
And could at any time, turn to dust.

Lived in the time of frozen world,
When snowflakes drifted and glaciers swirled.
Clear Ice sheets, and snow whiter than this page,
Scrawny calls that time, the Ice age.

On those cold winter nights,
My thick fur kept me cozy and warm.
And to those killers, who attacked in moonlight,
My tusks were enough, to deal them serious harm.

Though chances were slim,
Scrawny's ancestors, sometimes did win.
Then one day, I had a great fall,
It was the day, when nature killed us all.

Though once mighty, I'm still out of reach,
Reduced to Scrawny's, figure of speech!

3. Elephant :

Bless me, O' great Mammoth,
You are the hero of our lore.
I am also from Elephantidae family,
That's what my father told.

As the ice melted, I lost my thick fur,
Though the tusks were retained,
They still look different from yours.

I move through both streets and forests,
Gracefully through wind and rain.
Scrawny calls me gentle giant,
I was easier to train.

He trained me to carry lumber logs,
He rode me in his nasty wars.
I lost your wild aggression,
And then was used by them all.

Forgive me, O' forefather,
I know I have failed.
With these words of remorse,
I end my pity tale!

4. Tiger :

Greetings O' great Mammoth,
Apologies to intrude.
I am descendant of thy friend,
The mighty Sabretooth.

De facto king of this jungle,
I rule fierce and free.
I move like a shadow,
Almost invisible to anyone who may see.

With these stripes like fire, bold and black,
I blend in this environment, they don't see my attack.
In the shroud of darkness, if you see two glowing lights,
Those will be the eyes, of this assassin of the night.

With just my roar like a thunder,
I can put Scrawny on the run.
Coz, he knows for sure,
He can't face me without his gun.

Our numbers are now dwindled,
And though I am still as majestic as I once was.
Could still be gunned down for my skin,
For my canines and my claws!

5. Cobra :

Rest assured, O' king Tiger,
For many, you still dwell too far.
Only a few dare trespass your kingdom,
Even fewer, come too near.

But for me it's rather different,
As I roam in both these worlds.
Basking the sun here on this tree branch,
Or feasting on mice in Scrawny's ranch.

Scrawny calls me Cobra,
I am the Jungle's hooded knight.
I can strike faster than lightning,
And can kill with just one bite.

Across the nations and generations,
I am both revered and feared.
Though Scrawny has now developed an antidote,
But still my hiss is the last thing he want to hear!

6. Crocodile :

Hello there, king Tiger,
It's been a while.
Greetings to the great Mammoth, and to everyone,
From the ruler, in the depths of the Nile.

I am lord of the marshlands, and murky waters deep,
Hunting in a habitat, where shadows & whispers sleep,
You may have heard Scrawny call me by,
The name - ferocious mighty Crocodile.

Underwater, Undetected, I can silently swim,
And pull my prey in, when they come to drink.
It's always futile, to ever put up a fight,
Coz, my jaws crush all bones, with a single bite.

My skin is a gift, rough and tough,
A durable shield from nature's bluff.
And so Scrawny hunts me for that,
He likes to use my skin, to make his shoes and bags!

7. Wolf :

I sympathize with your sorrow,
I know how it felt.
As many of my friends were also,
Hunted for their silver pelt.

In cover of night, dark and cold,
If at all Scrawny, see me attack.
He knows the danger, is way lot more,
As we always hunt in a pack.

My distant cousin, long ago,
Somehow sought Scrawny and got too close.
Abandoning our ways, he left the woods,
And chose to be domesticated, for free food.

I have seen Scrawny manipulate,
Kill and mutilate, his own kind.
Will kill this earth, if he could,
And yet calls me, big bad Wolf!

8. Bear :

I was deep in my slumber, curled up for some rest,
Dreaming of springtime, and the sun at its best.
Then I heard some noises, whispers through the trees,
I haven't yet stolen any honey, so knew it won't be bees.

So, I crawled out of my burrow, and look what I found,
All my pals from jungle, debating on common ground.

Speaking of this Scrawny, he usually doesn't come near,
As I stand on my hind legs, he always trembles in fear.
When unarmed, he always run,
Screaming, "Look, it's a big black Bear!"
Once armed, he might return,
Possibly, for my thick fur.

My fur is like this dark earth, and eyes deep and wise,
Living my life slowly, I gaze at the open skies.
Mighty yet still humble, wild yet fairly pure,
Feasts on fish, fruits, nuts, and berries,
And some honey to lick and smear!

9. Panda :

I guess you all are wondering,
"Who is this fur ball?"
I'm Bear's distant brother,
But not ferocious at all.

In the bamboo forests, lush and green,
If you see a gentle giant, that would be me.
With black and white fur, I'm nature's teddy,
Scrawny calls me Panda, says I'm cute and cuddly.

You will usually see me, lost in the blue,
And almost always, munching on bamboo.
Then I sleep on a tree, but not too tall,
Coz when I roll, I usually fall.

My role is simple, my life is slow,
A peaceful soul, I go with the flow.
There was a time, when we were hunted,
But now Scrawny saves us, had us protected!

10. Parrot :

I'm just whistling,
Don't you all tag me with him.
I just mimic his words,
I wasn't involved in his deeds.

Grooving and exploring,
I'm just a jungle nerd.
When you hear me speaking,
You must admit, I'm the cleverest bird.

You have seen me in vivid colors,
Though I'm usually emerald dyed.
But its my gift of mimicking his words,
That caught Wingless's eye.

Intrigued by my ability,
He gave me center stage.
Then he took my freedom,
As he put me in a golden cage.

"Give me back my free sky", as I boldly cry,
He shuts me fruits & nuts, or some coconut pies.
Looking back at my life, I clearly lost this bet,
Now I'm just a living toy, just his talking pet!

11. Chimpanzee :

I can relate to Parrot,
As I've gone through a similar phase.
Though I have not put in a golden one,
Mine was just a bigger cage.

Scrawny calls me Chimpanzee,
Thinks he has evolved from me.
But that doesn't make much difference,
As he exploits my life for free.

But in my gaze, you'll see a spark,
Of something human, small but stark.
With intelligence of a toddler, I can grip and hold,
I have tender heart and a beating soul.

Here in the jungle, I play wild and free,
Swing from the branches, sway with the trees.
Life in the jungle is so much more fun,
Hope I don't hear, the sound of a gun!

12. Frog :

If the root of your sorrow, was just the cage,
You will be horrified by my case.
Parrot and Chimp, I meant no disrespect,
But my story has an even darker page.

Thousands of us, caught by that Giant,
Just to be slit, in the name of science.
I still don't know, why he needs to dissect me,
Even though I don't share his anatomy.

Yet here I live, in muddy embrace,
I'm called a Frog, with greenish grace.
With strong hind legs, I leap so high,
With a flick of my tongue, I catch a fly.

With eyes stretched wide, skin wet and bright,
I hop around in the pale moonlight.
My croaks echo, loud and clear,
Calling friends from far and near!

13. Deer :

If king Tiger decides to hunt me,
I'll have nothing more to say.
Coz he is the legitimate predator,
And I am his rightful prey.

But I can't say the same for Scrawny,
And that's what I want to report.
Unlike my majestic Tiger king,
For him, hunting's just a sport.

For year after year, we hone our skills,
To outrun the claws, to escape the teeth.
With his one lucky shot, we taste bitter defeat,
I hate when he boasts and flaunts these cowardly kills.

Scrawny calls me timid Deer,
Yet he is the one who is more vulnerable to fear.
If in the jungle, you feel a velvet touch,
That would more likely be my fur.

I adorn my antlers, as a crown of pride,
A symbol of my grit, where my strength resides.
Yet in my gaze, you'll find something more,
A softness, like the ocean's shore!

14. Butterfly :

With me, he plays a different sport,
Usually harmless, more on a lighter note.
As I fly around, his finger or face,
He seems to like it and give me a chase.

My life had been through many a phase,
Once a worm, then a tight-shut case.
But time and change gave way to sky,
And now I soar, for I have learned to fly.

I fly gracefully with my painted wings,
Through sunlit skies and meadow rings.
My colors spark in warm daylight,
A fleeting glimpse, then out of sight.

As a beautiful Butterfly, I am widely adored,
Yet sometimes, the Wingless pin me to boards!

15. Firefly :

O' Butterfly, truly in the daylight,
You are the star of the show.
But it's these warm nights,
That light up with my glow.

In velvet dusk, so soft and shy,
I'm a spark that sways in the sky.
A golden pulse, a fleeting flame,
I'm a speck of sun, with no heat to claim.

I move through air on silent wings,
A lantern borne by jungle beings.
When the Wingless, saw this flame in sky,
He started calling me, Firefly.

Too brief to catch, too bright to stay,
But you can follow me, I'll light up your way.
Smile when you see me, twinkle like a star,
Just don't let the Wingless, imprison me in a jar!

16. Bumblebee :

I can feel these conversations heating up,
And can see that everyone is quite worked up.
Let's take a moment to calmly diffuse,
While I finish sipping some flower juice.

I'm not like our friend, the Honeybee,
For I alone decide when I'm busy.
Flying with all my weight, is not that easy,
I'm a marvel of nature, Wingless calls me Bumblebee.

Buzzing through the morning light,
I'm a fuzzy speck in peaceful flight.
My velvet coat and tiny wings,
Are softer than a brush of silk.

From bloom to bloom, I hop all day,
With pollen dust, I mark my way.
And when I'm tired, I take a nap,
On a leafy bed, or in a floral shack!

17. Honeybee :

Yes, you're surely not like me,
Coz Bumblebee, you're just too lazy.
Being heavy and tired shouldn't be your quirk,
Try to move faster and don't sleep at work.

The way of the bee, should be through discipline,
To live for the hive and die for the queen.
With mud, wax, and grit, we build our honeycomb,
A majestic castle that we call our home!
We pollinate the flowers and take some nectar,
Store it in our castle, processed as royal treasure.
When the Wingless see this, it makes him so greedy,
He calls our treasure honey and calls me a Honeybee.

For many millennia, he came as an enemy at our doors,
To steal our treasure, to smoke us out—
And break our sacred homes.
We fight as one and make him run,
He's still afraid of getting stung!
Our strength lies in our numbers,
We don't hesitate, we don't pause.
For every winged trooper,
Sting and die for a greater cause!

18. Chameleon :

Very well said, O' Honeybee,
Just like a war-cry, it filled me with hope.
As every time, when I heard that Giant speak,
Words of deceit is all he spoke.

He fakes it all, he scams his folks,
But in the bad book, it's my name he invokes.
I'm not related—it's not my dominion,
Yet he calls all those untrustworthy—
A color-changing chameleon.

My eyes, like orbs, can see through thy soul,
Not just its color, but the true intentions it holds.
Slowly and steadily, I cautiously tread,
With sticky toes and tail outspread.

I don't need to roar, don't need to pace,
Like a ninja, I just blend in place.
The jungle's spy, the garden's mime,
I'm master of both, shade and time!

19. River :

I heard some strong noises, out here in the wild,
Seems y'all are complaining, about my Wayward Child.
So I thought I'd check it out, as I passed by,
Consider me your neighbor, flowing nearby.

I'm a timeless tale, both deep and long,
On an endless journey, flowing strong.
A quiet force, with ancient pride,
I carve through the mountains, tall and wide.

My waters shimmer, silver and bright,
Reflecting stars in the quiet night.
Quenching the thirst of millions as I flow,
Creating new life wherever I go.

As I flow from peaks to ocean's shore,
Not just clay and silt, I embrace much more.
He drinks, he sprays, he uses me to commute,
But my Wayward Child, has me pollute.

But still, I'll love; I'll always be a giver.
As he calls me, I'll always be a sacred River!

20. Eagle :

Flying above, when I took a look,
I saw down here, an unusual group.
I'm all ears, for some exciting scoop,
Hope y'all, aren't planning a coup.

You know me as bird, that fly so high,
With wings that stretch and brush the sky,
From mountain peak to valley deep,
Through roaring winds, I bravely sweep,

I'm a monarch, crowned in skies untamed,
By nature's law, my reign's still proclaimed.
With elegance unmatched, none can compare,
Wingless calls me Eagle, but honestly, I don't care.

Speaking of Wingless, I just saw him shout,
Trust me, it was him—I'm the jungle's best scout.
On the edge of the jungle, for a while, he stood,
Then, slowly with a heavy heart, he entered the woods.
Ask him your questions, don't judge him too soon,
Now it's morning—he'll probably reach here by noon!

21. Human :

Hello there, everybody, sorry I'm late,
It seems y'all have started, hope I didn't make you wait.
I can feel a deep tension here, I can see all your hate,
I'll hear your feedback, I'm open to debate!
I know you call me by nicknames,
As I walk the path of shame.
I'm that Scrawny, Wingless, Wayward Child,
And that mindless Giant you can blame.

8 billion of us walk on Earth, each with a different mind,
Evolution gave us intelligence, A true gift from divine.
But we took it for granted, didn't see those subtle signs,
Some use it to nurture the world, some use it for crime.

I came here to apologize, and will surely take all blame,
But believe me, when I say, not all of us are the same.
There are Humans who truly care,
Lend their helping hand, they protect and share.

And now to the fellow human, reading this book,
Thanks for making it this far and listening to this group.
May their stories inspire you in many ways,
And help you stay on the righteous path you take!